"Invite inside the arcane dawn / Hello." Alan Felsenthal's *Lowly* is quietly oracular. With feeling and purpose, these poems move through precise intensities of thought to lay bare an integrated sense of a possible world. With such paradoxes and subtleties, we might call Felsenthal a new Metaphysical Poet.

— SUSAN HOWE

Lowly is a gem: full of sly music & ancient wisdom & hilarious with timelessness, it makes tough & tender love to all the ages, especially ours. I have read it over & over.

— ARIANA REINES

LOWLY

Lowly
© Alan Felsenthal, 2017

ISBN 978-1-937027-87-2

First Edition, First Printing, 2017

Ugly Duckling Presse
The Old American Can Factory
232 Third Street #E303
Brooklyn, NY 11215
www.uglyducklingpresse.org

Distributed in the USA by SPD/Small Press Distribution
Distributed in Canada via Coach House Books by Raincoast Books
Distributed in the UK by Inpress Books

Cover Design: Ben Estes
Design and typesetting: Doormouse, emdash, & Tío Carlos
Type: Avenir and Bembo

Printed and bound in the USA by McNaughton & Gunn, Saline, MI
Covers printed at Prestige Printing, Brooklyn, NY

The publication of this book is made possible in part by the National
Endowment for the Arts, by public funds from the New York City
Department of Cultural Affairs in partnership with the City Council,
and the continued support of the New York State Council on the Arts.

LOWLY

Alan Felsenthal

CONTENTS

for Michael Silverblatt

I've given
you my
emptiness: it may
not be unlike
    your emptiness:
    in voyages, there
    are wide reaches
    of water
    with no islands:

— A.R. Ammons
Tape for the Turn of the Year

TWO MARTYRS

Two martyrs stalked the earth
almsgiving equally
so neither knew the other
was capable of competition
until the first martyr sacrificed
his life before the township
by jumping into a fire pit.
Some said the second martyr
inspired by his friend's decision
faced the pit and lit himself on fire.
After the first martyr saw this act
he was immediately resurrected
only to end his life once more
by lighting his body on fire
then jumping from the tower.
The town gasped as suddenly
the second martyr reappeared
afire and shaking the tower until
its shattered stones covered him.
This cycle of sacrifice went on
so long the two turned
into an attraction for travelers.
Soon they were no longer
considered martyrs
but brothers whose punishment
for misusing fire
was to continue misusing it.

HOLLY

We sat by the river till night.
What is night

we asked. The time we leave
the river. Like

the weir made out of brush and
boards, we caught the fish. And

brought its body home
in frosted plastic bags. How's

it structured, we wondered as
we reached inside for bones and

when we found the wishing one
that laughs when cracked, only

then we asked for day, which
we knew is where the river was.

ARGO

A hull made to touch
the arctic shoulder of the vacant
sea. And she is a ship who speaks
words learnt from water.
The half of her you can see
is the present tense.
Her wake is words.
Above, the gods have confidence
in what she says. Years are the stars'
sentence, aimed at your sail—
their incomplete sentence,
your half-made life. 26 stars
line the ship, each star lifts
its own weight like the letter i.
A little timber holds you up too,
speaks when you're not
listening. At times your timber
is light, the stern illuminated.
Other times, the overlong circle
of the sea points with its mist
upward, a rain nestling in the eye
of passing night, to an unchanging
station that blinks like a house
at your terror. It was a good deed,
your birth, and a reward is coming.
Not today, not tomorrow, soon.
The laughing winter, your hair
expires, a film distorts warm faces
you know you'll soon forget.

Even water will forget your skin.
The sun warts your ears' tips,
your lips too chapped to pray. You
who harbored a bull of guilt.
The bull will be appalled
to learn your sentence
spoken by milk in the heavens.
Rewards of human life are
wind without a coat, limbs
torn apart by neighbors, and
sometimes you're the thief.
The body in the well or resting
at the foot of an oak tree.
The half you cannot see
or hear was stolen. You arrived
on a ship, only one exists.
She spoke to you, to your grandparents,
but it was cold for everyone
and so they slept.

THE PROBLEM WITH RHYME

The problem of rhyme is not
what grandmother spoke
about when she talked
in her German accent.
What she meant,
the problem of Rhine,
sounded more like rime
frosting the banks.
Perhaps the problem
of Rhine had more to do
with rime than rhyme.
I asked if she confused
the words I used
with other words she knew.
This lapse expanded
with each utterance
the time it takes for what
one means to make pure
sense to the other.
                              "My mother
grew this stutter,"
she sighed, "I could not
understand it was words
until she died.
The problem with Rhine
is no river here stays
worthy of drowning.
When the righteous
leave a place, the place

is diminished,
and a woman is finished
who does not know
it is her time to swim.
When everywhere is
winter, there is
no time to consider
freezing, only the harm
in not staying warm."

SAILING BONES

Suffering I drifted to you
Seeing my suffering you suffered
Our conference on calamity
Our joints moved against wind
Sustained our growing pain
Until protruding bones
From our rumpled skin coats
Broke through to expose
Their staid, stagnant structures
To a cat we were dual cat castles
A bird perched upon my clavicle
To a friend traveling by
We no longer existed
But our suffering did

IF YOU NEED A RIDE

I bathed in the salt of the sea, the past lives within
me. The past raises, is raised, and my body

comes to know me as a boy. I know a boy
who died inside a man's body. I regard all men

I knew as boys, as boys. A woman carried him
almost a year and he grew to be unremarkable.

She didn't have to believe in man to create one.
Law stays law whether or not I drive licensed.

This car clinks as I drive my women hither,
they now prefer its cracked sound to conversation.

As bedchamber attendant, I offer a coffer of tears. Women
acknowledge my once great voice. I touch my breastplate—

there died the lamb I was. A wraith of twilight, he grazes
on gloom. Beams back in half-light what man cannot see.

The women, when a man steals from them things
not to be returned, sit with me. Nothing

returns as it left, even the pillar of cloud that saves
these words. On TV, I watched an owl encircle her nest

with clumps of shit the black beetles then pillaged.
Beetles consumed dried dung, owl chicks ate beetles.

It's easy to say our inheritance of shit sustains us,
given: your soul's the latrine you get to clean.

I am rubbing the salt in spirals over my body,
hoping what leaves is worse than what enters.

Turning to salt's not worse than eating shit. Lot's wife,
tired of Lot, lost her shoulder as she glanced over it

backward into sky-clad sulfur, from which she heard
the sound tomorrow cannot make.

The mountain, the radiated valley. The sheriff
of quickness, stretching day across its altar.

EL DORADO

A firefly committed to the orphanage
the night I graduated
and prayed for the petite kindness
unknown to an aiming hand
inside a shoe.

BEGINNING WITH A HORSE

A horse has six legs
two belong to a man
who might be Pluto
disguised as the devil
abducting a unicorn
whose horn was used
to purify a spring
that whetted the infinite
now behind us

ALTERNATE ZOO

A lawn is lit by souls asleep
in tandem or alone, or hiding in a hive
averse to soil, a crypt. Above
stands a crane who does not dance
around. His graceful leg is a sundial.

But what's the stone a crane holds while he bends
one leg? They say a stone keeps the crane
bent from ever dozing off. If it drops, it hits the bottom
of his other leg. But the crane really carries a
bee, which never stings the silent

crane, because it doesn't judge him for holding it close
so long. The crane, unlike us,
cannot dream of bees and, therefore, does not die—he caresses
the bee, whose spirit would rather wander, like ours, out of
      the still
cradle of the crane's

dark palm. These small actions of thought are daily
in the cemetery when one is not noticing
doves, who sing the song of a stone doorway.
A whole genre of song, once in books, for the good
death, which used to happen at home.

Everyone then knew how to die, even
if illiterate, and family
excursions to the cemetery were popular, like emblazoned
symbols. The parents woke their children

early to walk to the gates where the regardful

faces of Janus either let you in or forgot
to keep you out. His
four eyes weighed the soul like a scale and human hands
    held felt
flowers that could bob and dance,
float among the visitors like a parade of lanterns

greeting the stones that represent the greatness
of matter. The hardened
ground hardened itself, so graves
could not be dug very deep. Pebbles
go on top. The rock mounds

happened as grave markers by accident, should you happen
to believe in accidents. If a nomad
had to pass the gravesite of another tribe, he
might repair a plot by adding stones.
How did he know whose

it was wasn't a question he asked. If
it's too arid to cry, you can leave objects
instead—flowers (real), immortelles
(ceramic), toys, ten cents, and fallen
insects (especially the canty and

joyful water witch, a national emblem of the Japanese
island of Honshu, which some believe can

[25]

join the eyelids for the journey
ahead). But I shouldn't
just tell you of good things that help us sleep when the things

keeping us awake are as ageless. The King
of Terrors chimes the rusted
keys of Time and swings them as a scythe to harvest the
        souls of knights
and pharaohs alike, waiting outside a church,
kiosk of Trajan, east of the Nile in Egypt

leaning against lily-topped
columns that echo unfolding
life while two cobras answer with death, above papyrus leaves
for knowledge and rebirth. A
little more confusing when vulture wings symbolize

maternal care. Not as baffling as the pelican, who might
be feeding her babies from a pouch
many believe to be her flesh, a common mistake,
as though babies eat blood for anyone but the dreaming
martyr. Craftsmen built the birds of prey and it's impossible

not to suffer as a symbol. Next
is the woodpecker, an able storm-predictor, who would
not help God make trenches for rivers and lakes. Now
he is a headbanger, though Romulus and Remus
needed his food delivery services

often when making Rome. There's the owl
who hates light and never cries when crying
offers the only neutralizer of poison. Once
upon a time before our eyes were rocks, before the columns broke
off and fell into the center of the earth, the whole family

produced tears together, not as a trick or decorative device but
    to pacify
the soul leaving the house, to tell them that water yields
plants and the daffodil finds light in paradise
as often as in the underworld, where no pagan soul is
poor, wrapped in clovers. One

question the youngest has quite
often: *are they coming back?*
Queen of Heaven never returns them. There are more questions
about her crown, its magical
qualities, and whether she

really kisses each soul goodnight. Nothing at night is reliable.
The spotted sky is an aviary for our imaginations of
real ones. The pathway to the sun is filled with burning eagles,
    redeemed
by plunging back into the waters of the tiny
red earth. The sacred eagle, it is

said, no matter his hunger, was so
generous he left half his prey for other creatures and
sometimes had twin heads. Though perhaps somewhere

each unacquainted
single-headed eagle was leaving

the other half for his discarded twin.
As the eagles fell back to Earth, like
torches inverted, they threw themselves
into the Nile with the desire of a lover
that listens to the blossom of a pansy to

understand the lost thoughts of her beloved. The smell under
flowers: drowsiness. Some symbols remain
unasked about, like seedpods and buds, which when broken usually
represent infants. How
unfortunate to see the lamb look upon the day's eye covering

vaults, sealed from experience, so the daisy never varies
from being a ceaseless
vigil for innocence, not a variation
of loves me / loves me not, which is
very foreign to a baby, who should never

wonder about these things. We
start again
with the crane, which
led to families and
what they do with tears. None of this is exact.

Yew trees give a maze of shade when you
sleep beneath the creeping boughs

yellow with buzzing, mutant yawns
from a tower of the winds, which toward
youth calls.

ENSUE

Regret cures desire
for immortality. I blink, the eye
amulet can't.
               If reliefs can, relieve.
               I can't relive
that week of funerals. Horizontal
tree, leaf urn, release my friend.

If I ever lie like that, a lid missing,
all dim signs, I give you permission
to retain no impression.

Retina, inert.

★

Her face in me remains. I lack the inverse
of seeing.
          Vision: ensue.
                    Do what you do
incautious. I dreamt I had a friend.

My therapist and Coleridge agree
I still do.
          I can easily believe invisible friends
in the jelly of my eyes float, flash. One can

unsee what one forgets. Now let me forget.

ALPHABET

I was a victim of laughter.
They set the alphabet
like a river
into which the names of God
bound by letters
sank.

I was dumb
for they called me so.
I smelled
water and lime
when I searched
for love
and watched
smart men sign
their names in smoke
over the ovens of Niesse
the poorest women
burned inside.

When I woke centuries after
the oven still alive
I remembered my father
said the devil was no cloud
of black flies
but an educated man
who lived by two hands
that invented the devil
to give him human help.

The devil heard this
and cried
not out of sadness
but to try
something new.
I cried too
for now I knew
not what crying
meant.

'BUT THE BIRDS DIVIDED HE NOT'

The albatross has been abused by poets
by being compared to them.

Poet's goat.
Not through gates of the temple
led by priests, passed
from booth to ceremonial booth,
does the albatross await sacrifice.
Sea is the anteroom.

The sea, spool of junk, similar to land
abides by plastic the albatross eats.
A lighter in a jug, submerged fire-
crackers. Shiny streams of steadfast blue
overlap the wave's face, oily as fish
eggs to the albatross eye.

At the nest, a sandy trash disc, baby
feeds upon polymer lanyard, molds
its own belly into an altar.
The beach shelters the ribs
of chicks once they burst with plastics.
By maggots their confetti shivers.

The maggots say:
Ye shall be clean.
The poets look dirty as yesterday.
They go home and attempt to split
a mussel through metaphor.
Their beards left to grow, grow.

MY DOMESTIC POEM

The remedy for your ruminations is bedbugs.
When you acquire bedbugs
you are blessed
for you only have one problem,
like when you're addicted to drugs.
When you're addicted to drugs
your problem is being addicted
to drugs. And bedbugs, like drugs,
divide your life.
You are thinking of them when you're not
thinking of yourself. Thinking of yourself
leads to rumination, your reaction
to distress involving bedbugs.
Look upon your life as not bare
when you consider theories.
You do not live a bare life,
one without rights. An exception,
the bedbug is a daemon,
a nymph sent, like a dream, to connect you
to a history of visual communication;
for we understand as much about invisibility
as we do DSL technology.
The shadow of the bedbug remains
on your sheets when they are white,
like calligraphy from other worlds,
ideograms writ in shit
instead of clay, which seem to convey
that bedbugs, like Sumerians, are responsible
for one of the earliest systems of writing.

A bedbug smashed on its mattress
signs its will in your blood,
the way they did centuries ago
with the limbs of kings and gods
who took the form of human beggars.
Beggars who did not own freezers,
like mine, filled with clothing removed
when I got home from the movies.
I shook my pants over the bathtub.
Then folded, I slid them
between my jacket and shirt
where, if I had any, ice cream should be.

Amanda asked me to write this poem.
She said, *write about something*
you do every day, something domestic.
I go to the grocery store when I can't
make eggs with what's in the fridge,
but I fill my freezer with clothing
as often as I leave the apartment.
My rite. I signed a contract with life
that states: a chair covered in fabric
is a divine throne of the city you visit
when sitting down, and when you go
you leave with an echo of that seat.
Once I brought a bedbug home.
The proportion of its body to mine was nothing
compared to its power upon my thoughts.
They use the stars and clouds and wind

to guide their way into your mind.
When you Google *what does a bedbug*
look like pictures, you are not Googling
yourself. In an image, the brown back
of a fifth stage nymph shines
like a mushroom
intoxicated by the effulgence of wet dirt.
Is mud the timetable of blood?
Mud is the roof of the underworld.
The underworld's unpeopled palace
is colder than I thought, but nothing wretched
belongs there. If nothing is wretched,
thoughts misled me with my permission.
The bedbug is where it belongs, a body
was built to be vanquished. Trust the lovers
of beds and bodies. We hardly know
whom we've slept with. Somewhere else
a mosquito survives August by killing
a child who just learned cursive.
They don't teach cursive anymore.
The coldest moment of morning
is when I put on my jeans, especially my thumb
touching the button. During that ecstatic instant,
looking at its imprint on the frost,
I think only of usefulness.

LAW

The lair of despair lies inside the law.
Grandma knew, gangsters know.

Don't let them convince you though
your heart is said to lodge gold.

A goldsmith sold might—
might ghosts the old.

True power gilds the moth, most
haled then forgot like a loathed toad.

Hide hearts of gold in the fogged open,
lead forth, go. Fog, the Lord's heat,

is hate of the ogler. They consume
earth, that herd gold. Loot is drool,

age-old froth. One law drags the slight,
the other odor is the flag, my dear bylaw.

ON LEARNING OF THE HOLY STONE UNAKITE, SAID TO CLEAR THE HEART FROM CRAVING THE DEPARTED, I WANTED TO FILL MY HEART WITH UNAKITE

Identification by emotional gravity,
I am my own gemologist.
In my skull no oil spills;
I wrap my hands around its rock,

to shake until my eyes turn in-
to snares for the good image.
The earth splits and I go
to its part to speak to the ex-gods

who hold up the tottering earth
with horns, unmusical horns,
with lowly names,
which each resemble stars

though they reside underground.
These counted names I can't
tell you without obscuring
their glory with clouds of

false breath, tears.
Fathers of beasts
flee tears. A heart
feels ill set in snot.

So to be the beast doomed,
seal the envelope of
splendor. Pharaoh
spoke to me, commanded: gore

your foe. In days of
yore, you smashed people and,
yon, sent them away. Heads wagged,
yet they sang the songs the nation sang,

sunk with shame into a
single consonant: y.
Somewhere between yah and yeah, they
sounded like cymbals.

Then I put down my bow and
the arrow of my illness.
They fled. Like the sea,
there was nothing wrong with them.

IF THERE IS NO MIŁOSZ

Or if there is no God, not
everything is ironic.
A poet still has a sister
and is not permitted to sadden her
by saying he is God.

PSALM

This will take a glacial slumber, to move
my foot for it suffers. When my foot suffers
I suffer and nothing less than sleep, different
from slumber, can take my eyes. In my heart
is a heifer, her dust, ashes that purify
my heart for touching a corpse. I touched
a corpse and it was my own, and since
then all I can do is slumber. Make amends.
'Tis a fairy world inside my bones, keening
there in the world of ash is an ardent gleam,
which waits for polish like a smile. Make
a hill and keep it for the hope of help.
Never let the heavens, their earth, leave
you without help. Say I was just a boy
then and now I can hear the question.
Where is the water that bathes blemishes,
how can I get it to the heifer in my heart?

LIKE SOMEONE ONCE WAS

In myself I will call my soul a she, and to her be singular.

The chains brought pain upon my leg.

I wanted to start with pleasure.

In another dream I will have before death, unity shines inside a fable. A fable in which twins die and are born again conjoined, and only then do they share their opposite natures. But they do not remember their natures, because they have been born again. One could do nothing outside agony; the other lived in a pleasuredome. They must follow each other now. Without each other, they have no names.

I wanted to be a composer. My dreams told me so.

"Cultivate." They said. "Make music."

I was already making music, so I figured I might as well enter a contest, since I'm dying. This should be a popular hymn. Hymns honor, shouldn't they? I would like to honor a color that only exists after death.

I invent stories. Out of other stories. I can only repeat what I have heard.

A scruple is the enemy of a moment.

One day we will understand the opposite of life.

Often I pondered two knobs separated by their door. My dreams whispered to me about them. They are helpless, like a man. If they ask you to remove their door, you have no right. They can never possess each other in this life.

I rejoice my summoning.

I am a good man to her, I am her man. I will take the poison twice or more. The debt shall be paid; that is all.

I tried to see and hear the truth before I became a poet. Did anyone ever earn perfect vision?

The body wants a dollar. It looks for money in the food of war.

She wants to leave his body, to be alone.

All I love is knowledge. The pleasure of which I am intemperate.

The cone-tipped staff twined with ivy does not tempt me. They are many.

I want to recollect my mysticism. But are the thyrsus-bearers, if by nature generated by their opposites, the true mystics? If I can remember the moment before I forgot, I will know I am a mystic now.

The misanthrope denies experience. That is the sting I leave before dying.

A man can be equal to a lyre. His beloved used to play songs. I know myself as his garment. But I never knew him.

Dear children, I will always repeat myself until I cannot. Meantime, let me be the charmer. The sky is so calm we could die in it.

Within the next invisible world, withdrawn from the absence of light, I am no longer a drunkard. Myself gathers into myself.

Her eyes, being rivets, fasten her firmly to the haunted body.

Let my old hands pat the locks against your neck.

Have I convinced myself?

My first principle was made to hold up the second.

I am speaking like a book, but I believe that what I am saying is true.

I could not look at things. Out of fear that seeing was a sense and senses make the world a vortex. The earth seems to balance without the crutch of air.

If only I had been a fish. I grew tired of swimming and one day, popping my head through the limit of the sea, saw the world beyond. This hollow of earth, streaked like a leather ball, was not the only surface. I grew wings and flew to the top of the heavens, then looked down at the sea, which was now stupidly filled with brine. But the luster, radiance of an unnamed color. Sitting inside the corroded caves were friends, twins who knew nothing and could learn nothing from me now. The true light is the loneliest light there is.

Crimes and the brothers of crimes are not her attendant genius. She will be led into a proper room without a body. This is the only room that fits.

I walked about. My legs failed in chains.

I serve the swans and cannot love money. My song lusts for the votary.

There is no bed, be quiet, have patience. A voice is calling.

Crito, let someone take her home.

CRITO, OR I HAVE NOTHING TO SAY

Socrates: "The power of the people
is randomness. They tie us to a wheel
the bogies spin, which rakes our minds
with the song of chains
and is called property." I felt these

words within my ruined
body. My reason is a pair
of children, who court contempt by making
decisions. Again Socrates talks to the Laws.
Never knew another country.

Come to Thessaly, I said it once. The thought
escaped my mouth like the runaway
in a shepherd's smock. This country will make
foreigners of his children. I will follow,
listening to their angry grunts
as though the strains of music.

PSALM FOR UPRIGHT VISIONS

I met a man who knew my name, delivered
a *Euphorbia milii* to my home. At noonday
the righteous plant flowered a thousand
pink eyes and looked upon me wickedly. Sing
to me, said the plant, the song that moves
the world and wilderness to rejoice—sing
of the blood that, as it sings, is turning
back to water. I am hardly ever thirsty and
my soul abhors meat, the plant said, here
is all the fruit I can assemble; take, take
the fruit and praise it as though weak
from fasting; lift your head and hearten
for you praise the soul keeping your feet
from falling. I opened my lips and stood
upright—my mouth, a mischievous device,
sang of a man who knows my name, my eyes
toward his from my window. And when
he looked back I ended my little ice age,
his lips moved too and I tried to assemble
the words like a broken vessel. His eyes
saw my sandy substance and yet he spoke.
I can conceal knowledge, but my heart swears
diligence to sadness.

                              The heart's ambassador
is never too perverse. It goes into the warmth
of the tabernacle to praise a footstool. Make
my soul at ease with my heart's contempt—
make my soul my heart's footstool.

THE LADS OF ATLANTIS

The young tear away like a river
              cannot love a god
Beyond the oak and linden tree
              a better world awaits
the world in which the seed of being
              someone vanishes
A pageant where I love
              aslant
The forest's portcullis unlocks
              parades of beloved scents
to which David plays the lyre in Palestine
              I am not allergic to art
in which David begets
              music
like wind through whale bones
              on an undocumented beach
such estranged notes the whale becomes
              whole again
and shelters Jonah with her warmth
              At the pageant
Abraham drinks through the testing
              dancing on the vine-trellis
Atlantis is his gate nap
              The donkey waits on Abraham
Isaac soft shoes over the altar
              under which he might have slept
Now the mouths of a pear cloud babble
              into rays that blind Abraham
as the donkey lowers his ears

they learn of judgment

Why not debate for the donkey

for the donkey came forward

and was fifty

if he was ten

If Atlantis

is not for Isaac then

give us the donkey

for a son

I wanted to be everything

nothing visits like a native village

If we grew up elsewhere

a palace of congenital deafness

to love

a lion's claw crooking the timber

no great love sets straight

Great lovers left us

Or were they nymphs

or were we

before a tree

began our current history

If we grew up elsewhere

where races are lost

in which Atlantic usurped Atlantis

the lariat we felt without seeing

while the forest winked

from its seventy faces

as something above might

                    facing down
Somewhere nothing precarious
                    lifts its cloudy crown
a grayish everlasting flower
                    dried and unfading
opens like this city
                    one night from a lessening distance
Even a better world awaits
                    a better world
Keep your world
                    for it was yours
If love be dumb
                    shhhhh, be dumb

TRANSLATION OF A LOST ARIA

None of the friends spoke until he spoke and asked the friends to kill him, lest he kill himself. *Enough,* they said in unison; *this is the United States, you cannot just go around asking to be killed.* He asked again. His voice was so beautiful that each friend considered it more. Though without training, he sang his request. The tone was like a ton of sorrow being lifted by a small tongue. Each listener in danger of weeping, incapable of leaving for the need to hear the end, which sounded like the remedy to its oblivion. *My body is made of sublunar stuff—it is a ruined thing—and to the sky I must return,* he sang. All of the friends had mothers and wondered what they might think of their sons for considering the killing of a boy who sang like a nightingale. *You had no choice,* a mother said, *the moon you were born beneath had written this in the yard with light the night you were conceived.* The friends touched each other and the heavens shone like mud. *Which of you has the knife?* They all had knives. It should come as no surprise the mud was really blood and through it emerged a star that pulsed with the voice of the boy. Mesmerized, the friends forgot his song while he ate their knives.

THE MIND'S ELOQUENT HOTEL

So I was told I sound like an 80-year-old.
Through my pen a curtained sea urchin
of Egypt reproduced the same hour
a tree blossomed on the Mediterranean shore.
In the olive tree a bird I invented stares
at anything not a worm as if the ocean.
My middle ear is melancholy and
some twink told me I'm sex negative
for not caring more about a starlet.
Both seem to be the case. Hiding
within a world order, between the mind
of here and Heaven, my Platonic year
in the shelter of symbols, I can easily forget
my own body, close friends in pain far away,
by imagining a state of timeless rest, the twigs
gathered outside the cave, where
she hasn't been seen for centuries. Inside
the moss is still moist. If the State watches,
a hero will not cry. She goes inside the cave
to become a small rock in the dark room
imperceptible as a bat. A white window,
the senator of night, and she shared
a long friendship, more intimate than touch.
Did I mean to use 'heroine'?
Without heroism, I hardened my heart
in an elaborate plot: the effect was a stern
old man with a scythe as his uniform,
just hanging inside me like a bone.
Poor guy. Is that sexual? Well, neither

was the worm I mentioned earlier
for the scarlet bird. I don't want
what I'm susceptible to, so don't come
for television when you visit. And yet I would
have been different, like God, if I couldn't
just do what all you could understand.
I poked a worm with a twig
the wind made shudder, the wind
I invented to stop me from poking the worm.
A bird from the sea alighted here to rescue
him from my hand, that wrote for this.

MALVOLIO

Revenge bends centuries as Malvolio
strolls on the stage of a modern play—
where he went when he left us.

No, he doesn't stroll. His death
knell was "done" that ended the song
a fool sang to please you. To want

to be pleased each day is greed.
'Tis true, 'tis true.
I once thought to baffle was to shame.

I met a man who begged because
a poverty of kindness addicted him
to pursue its surfeit glory, for Cressida

begged. And though not money poor
his world was full of fog, the kind that binds
itself to mirrors. Who calls him a lunatic?

Who calls me? I also laughed at the fool
but am no better than Malvolio
in jail, thinking of the soul as noble.

THE ATLAS OF ATLANTIS

Like a pigeon, I searched for discarded scraps upon the floors of the rich, to make with their nutshells and fish bones a map of the Holy Land. A map unreadable to the rich. To their eyes its value is like a sunken island, a shoal of mud, a tale before money. If the tale is told correctly, Atlantis appears through a division in the earth and I, a pigeon, am restored to the seat of an aged priest in the temple of Sais. Meanwhile, I shit white; and only the rock doves, preening to my song, drunk on water, know that though I sleep on twigs, I am a poet.

PSALM TREES

The god that writes a letter
sleep mails
sows our lids with images

I dreamt a twin
who dreamt my dream
which did not mean
the same to her

She had my mouth and
taught it how I speak
to fool myself

She convinced me to
conceive the angel
all things undisturbed
owe their unwanting

IN ALL CASES DROUGHT HAS THE SAME RESULTS

Sad numbers survive in place
of rainfall, produced by the same
declining area of pasture. Soil
has something to do with acts
committed, much like overgrazing
problems we find around
boreholes. Someone hears soul
in soil, as desertification rings
with decertification. What is
a village level to a regional one.
No, really, what is a village?
It can hardly become more
desert-like, selected for key
difficulties when annual rains
have failed, are late coming,
become smaller than water
received in recent years.
Overcultivation takes a number
of forms in our dry estimate,
some knowledge denuded
to divest a covering faster
than it can be formed. Clouds
condense into a liquid vertical
reality, and in the never still
air plants die or like us, live
in a water balance model
best defined by rainfall alone.

NOTHING ATTACKED WANTED TO BE

They didn't mean "follow your dreams" literally.
Even my alarm clock is anxious. The digits genuflect.
Headline says kneeling zealots. A boy playing
with a rat near an explosion leaves
all rats alone. Unknown, in Hebrew, means "not yet traumatic."
Like we're all freed now, like, because of Wi-Fi, we're free of the
    Sphinx?
What, my Lord? Oh, nothing. This video.

See. It's not that they'd do anything to be blind to misery;
they're blind to misery, so they do anything.
What is tender now? How does it feel
inside to wind in wool the breastbone's branches
not deafen its ears with its own explosives,
the soul's infirm trumpet.
Only to you your pain is famous.

Brooklyn kids in Berlin stole my inheritance to make projects.
I'm here, Prince, my kinsman, to ask truth if it has any power.
You're senile, he says. Think we're beyond oracles? Oh, Google
is men who milk the world, *the entire subhuman world*.
Is it they, out of chaos, coming to annul a mystic?
Or a tentative, sacred ghost in a vest of gold approaching;
he is a shy giant; he is light.

IF I COULD CALL A POEM FOR LOVE

To learn of love
from one who can't
being unloving
tell you why

why not love
him if while
while trying
to turn from

your reflection you
see a hand
reach out
where none is

WOOD

We enter a wood.
What is the dark—waves?

Warning? The time light
tilts its leaves?

The dark wishes for all
brightness to be equal, absently.

Bondable to rays of dark,
sodden and lost, dreamers

shear the shadows of hopes.
Invite instead the arcane dawn. Hello.

Invent past light. The woods
wink and it's day. We

wink, ancestors blushed. Offer
them a denser nest. They ate scorn. Offer

tenderness, whistle
wages of sorrow. Woodwind.

PAST LIFE PALINODE

A field theory sings its song
in the solid sphere of an astrolabe.
In the ancient tooth fished from an inlet,
in my great-grandfather's Islamic proto-clock
with the dials of the sun and moon.
When I remembered the sun was born
I forgot the name of an old woman
I used to visit on Sundays. My memories
are unrelenting, not rational. But
I grew up in a cult of personalization.

An all-embracing sea is reluctant
to give up the dead, centuries of wayward
ships, and mothers lost in transit. I suppose
all the tabletop paintings of Jerusalem
are underwater where there is no night
but eternal night. I wander a masculine
form for the half-feminine lord who knows
no last judgment. It's a double-lion,
a snake circling itself, a new sun setting
on the god who eats his children.
Harriet was her name. I was too afraid
to call the hospice when I moved.

Matter danced with glory and inside
my claw I held some precious sand.
A snake sees the world in hourglasses
on the way to a sacrificial meal for two.
If Oceanos ever ate dinner, he ate the snake-souls
after slaying his friend, the bull.

I'm not expecting to become the gate-
keeper of these mysteries. I only want time to read,
to feel a story well, stare at my beloved
and make of all my discomfort a household
shrine. A waterclock too has moods of love.
The hands of little girls pour water from above.
The music of time is measured in combustible powder
during a long shower with a man you come
to love. The burning of it might be a model
of creation and, like regret, irreversible.

I only want to know enough of the Zodiac
to stay away from Berlin. The surface
of a primordial ocean, hard and pitiless,
bubbles with the aeonic life of a god.
The son of a sun god—was his shadow gold?—
became identical to his father.
They held the thigh of a slain bull
over their heads until, a sun disc, it rose
a bone to the horizon. This was high summer
in Leo, blood dried as it dripped the moment
I figured out the sun gives gifts that include
illness. I was placed as a gnomon in the field
and stood until I finally felt. I desired
to cry for the right reasons. To concentrate,
I tried Saturn, the slowest visible planet, rules
the boundaries, the god of the sick, crippled
and creative, basically the lives of saints.
I never knew much about her life before
I visited, and now we have a chemistry

of symbols. As ghosts do, she asks *who
are you?* When she asks, I am a stranger
who edits the rhymed dirty jokes of the
Middle Ages for my imagined little sister.

If it ends, our own time, in general
cataclysm; if the reign on the right strives to
be the sun; if no brazen serpent on a rod ever
hisses again. Well I wanted to be more than
a breathing clock, not the tones of eternity,
the small dance of a worm whose moves
hollow out a hazelnut. So my steps form
dreams for the children I won't have, to give
to each other. My wife swings on the arc of a
cycloid and my husband, after playing skittles
on a fairy hill of giants, comes home an old man.
It's night, the trenches are filled with mysterious
friezes of light. I thought I had been here already
in my emotion–time diagram, in my field work,
in the letters I wrote and carried through
the circular river of the underworld, with my
suave mind awaking to life's errors, a garbled
painting, a painting in which what is whispered
is garbled, is the providence of irreversible
existence. Time's triads touched the soul as
the thread of life caught our ankles. I ran away.

Hurts less to speak in living images, to look
at the Sphinx and think of the sun strangling
the sky. To leave the royal tomb unguarded

for an hour, to tinge gold coins with river.
Like Hesiod said, *the hours are gods.* More
here than the kingdom of dwarfs, the hours,
barbers of amaryllis and Queen-Anne's-lace,
flowers from an Alice Notley poem. I was
working for poetry when I first noticed
only ordinary time is perishable. How did A
B C D and I appear in the same place at once?
I almost believe I could die
in a war or on the table of Solomon. I'm tired
of tricks. The sundial in the garden is either
a stylized tree or spinal cord of a sun god.
A spiral petroglyph dreams
of snakes, its shed skin imagines birth.

What I disown owns me. Time,
the hermit hunched to turn his hour-
glass, mine, and the blindfold I wore
to decide whether I could live
the sensual life. One century sees in
a blindfold justice, the next ignorance.
The same painting glistens like a lantern
waving, level to your eyes. Saturn
has no telephone, calls from the desert
to say the Sun lives: *time is okay now,*
somehow contemplation repairs you.
I tried to repeat *great, great, great*
and then tired of *great, great, great*
a god wafted its name amidst. I heard:
preserve the space between letters

for the fertile exclusion of sense.

Last weekend, I stayed home but denied
village life, rejected the details of a household
shrine, of Egyptian papyrus with two lions
whose support of the newborn sun god, who
withers plants without deep roots, offers a
double stance of dedication more active than
my own. To say each day we are given
a new God increases blasphemy, though
it also can be helpful. I volunteered to watch
old women sleep among flowers, I slept
curled at the foot of their obelisks.
I volunteered, so I guess I don't work here.
Jean-Luc Godard said, *the money, meaning*
the time, meaning having the money
and being able to spend it according to one's
rhythm and one's pleasure. To languish
unhumiliated, a victory. The stars care
less about their viewers than the drone
operators theirs, but looking obeys desire,
hope that one more thing might exist
than ten thousand, with earthly time to see.

The garbled voice of the animal from the
painting tells of divine time, like a pearl
beginning in the dragon's mouth, drowned
on its way to America. Time was born in
time, for time exists if America is not the soul
wherein a god is born. At the USPS,

I saw the forms of time give rise to
human venom in flux like the flow of grains.
A man yelling at a woman about his insights
into labor. He said: *we all work for the city.*
As though the city were a lotus or water
lily giving gods life, an umbel for order.
I had a thought from China in which, upon
uniting two opposite desires, an extratemporal
godhead, blowing salt into a void, births
the stillness in which everything happens
in one single, synchronous time, to be
recorded years from now on the badge
of an emperor's surcoat.

I dipped my finger in the Styx and—
spoiler alert—I don't understand love.
If matter explodes to no heat death, all sight
is circles and clocks, and no love lives
in the heavens, or love is created, destroyed
with no beginning or end, well—
instead we can focus on the light
clock of Al-Jazari, which burned
for thirteen hours. A pennyweight fell
each hour from within the candle,
to touch the figure who trimmed
the wick out by the time you slept.
The velocity of sleep is Einstein's theory.
It's like this: the temporal indication
of love is relative to the position of an
observer, watching her beloved sleep.

Careful where you aim your intensity.
When the moon in demon hands is closed,
they strike their pots and pans to distract
the demon. The moon makes music through
the fears of my neighbors. A pot, a pan,
the ancient hand of music in an orb.
If the lecherous wind has made us sick,
the moon will have its day.

The magic mirrors of Pythagoras measure
the moon in the breath of my beloved.
The moon lives as long as metaphor.
Looking east in a mirror, I viewed myself
as a harmonious snake. I sailed the boat of Ra,
on deck I walked a circle of archetypes.
My soul sat sweetly in the soft stern.
The boat of Ra, it sails above and below the
Internet. The boat which is a scepter, which
is a key the keeper of a gate sails into summer
with. The god of light, who bleeds helium,
whose sadness drips along the metal rods
peasants held to light new torches. That god,
living in a strobe, meant the majesty of night
was ours to see as we wanted. Outside
of books is not what we couldn't imagine.

The world-soul is not looking for us,
for the world-soul needs no fame.
Celebrity is the prayer of capital.
I was born under a falciform moon,

sickle shaped, and a stupor like a demon
makes me say the opposite of what I feel.
Keep your chart to yourself.
It's like giving away your last four digits.
Under the aromatic stones, near the Delta,
I wrote sentences with branches
I threw into the river wending to a sea.

Quietness failed and so I chose words.
Dear Sphinx, will this be my last bed
before the final visages I know sink
into the heavens? I hope to clearly say without
riddles, riddles of riddles, how it felt to live.
Between ego-time and aeonic time, on the way
to the timeless center, I ride
a slow-moving ibex with fiery eyes—mine,
not his. Fortuna shakes with monochromatic hands.
Our peacock ethics won't be seen,
for where she's expected, in total blindness,
in the center of a wheel, is nothing—
but that nothing rotates like nothing else.
I'll write to you from there.

THE LAST TRACES OF BLUFFS
FADING OUT

Once this same landscape was feral
then it became subdued
and in humans this could not but
be sad, as if a will
to retain sharp and uneven
ridges could impersonate a heart,
maybe more than once tricked
by the mind. Weathering rain-wash,
the river wears a waste apron,
grades the rocks to steeper slopes,
grows moss of a saintly hue.
I can't give you the infinite
details, though detail would show
I know a thing well, not broadly
convex hills and mountains, but fine
textures of ravines and spurs, the red
sandstone that turned to a torso
I saw in the old museum. The medium
and coarse domes, sugarloafs, the Sierra
Nevada of California, and the New
Zealand rocks of Tararua Range,
mantled with residual clay.
I never went there and still can
say the summits are of subdued
form, the relatively weak rocks
betray the resistant, or
the opposite, by their nearness
on the hillside slopes, varying

in exhibitions of the unending.
The infantile shoulder or edge
of the valley divides, and is
not ashamed of memory.

ACKNOWLEDGEMENTS

Some of these poems have appeared in *The Brooklyn Rail, Critical Quarterly, Elderly, Fence, Harper's, Hue & Cry* (New Zealand), *jubilat, Maggy, The Missouri Review, Poems by Sunday,* and the anthology *Still Against War: Poems for Marie Ponsot.*

"Lads of Atlantis" is for Marie Ponsot, whose blessing for this book—"a journey that forwards us"—has upheld me.

Special thanks to Dan, Emmalea, Camilo, Matvei, and the entire UDP team. And thanks to Ben for this beautiful cover.

Alan Felsenthal runs a small press called The Song Cave with Ben Estes. They co-edited *A Dark Dreambox of Another Kind: The Poems of Alfred Starr Hamilton* (The Song Cave, 2013). *Lowly* is his first collection of poems. He lives in New York.